From Here
Across the Bridge

From Here
Across the Bridge

Evelyn Klein

Woodcuts by
Wolfgang Klein

Nodin Press

Acknowledgements

The following poems have been published previously: "The Agate, Summer Evening" in the *Central St. Croix News;* "Interval" in the *Resources Management Newsletter of the University of Wisconsin–River Falls;* "The Navigator" in the *UW-RF Prologue.*

A special thank you goes to my son, William Bader, for technical support. Thank you, also, to my brother, Gary Klein, for his support and encouragement.

ISBN 13: 978-1-932472-42-4
ISBN 10: 1-932472-42-8
Library of Congress Control Number: 2006929684

Nodin Press
530 North Third Street
Suite 120
Minneapolis, Mn 55401

For my parents,
Wolfgang and Henrietta Klein,
and my children,
Angie and Bill

Introduction

Like a butterfly emerging from its cocoon, *From Here Across the Bridge* represents, for me, a coming of age. At a certain point in my life, the need for expression became overwhelming, and I returned to college to study for a masters degree in the Teaching of English. At the university I renewed my discourse with the outside world and also my inner search. When I eventually told my parents that I was going to make writing my future, my father's immediate response was, "I don't know what took you so long."

My mother, who had always been an avid reader, enjoyed reading my poems right from the start. Her grasp of what I was striving for amazed me, and she often discerned subtle references to events in our lives that she could understand better than anyone. She liked it when I wrote about my life.

When I first urged my dad to read the book, he shrugged his shoulders and said: "I don't know anything about poetry." I urged him to read it anyway. Even as a young child I had engaged in lengthy discussions with him—we talked about everything; nothing was off limits. Granted, the break-up of my marriage was a difficult topic. But this was a time of great change, where old traditions began to erode, and I wanted my father's input no matter what it was.

My father was the visual artist in the family. He saw things as no one else did and often came to conclusions ahead of the times. He first showed me how to look at the world up close, to see what it was really made of, that it was not just a blur we noticed in passing. In the lively discussions we had, he was the guiding star. Sometimes, when I showed him a poem, he would respond with, "Well, I know all that." When I countered with, "I have to write it anyway," he fully approved.

After he read the completed manuscript, his response was totally unexpected. "Boy," he said, "this is not only a story—it's a whole life's story." As if to affirm his words, he added: "Now you will need some illustrations for your book." But what came next made me ecstatic. "You could use some of my woodcuts," he suggested. What a vote of confidence! My father considered his woodcuts to be his most important life's work. He would work on them for months at a time, and never exhibited them anywhere except at museums, art institutes, libraries, or academic institutions. I was overwhelmed. My father, the accomplished artist, had offered me the greatest gift of all.

After he had sent me photographs of his woodcuts, the process of selecting pictures began. Many of my father's woodcuts could be topics for writing in and of themselves. The ones I eventually chose for *From Here Across the Bridge* are intended to reflect the story as it progresses. Many of them were created in Wisconsin, which is fitting, because many of the poems were also written against that backdrop. Come to think of it, one of them used to hang on my bedroom wall when I still lived at home. Once, in the middle of the night, it fell off the wall with a big crash, startling me out of a deep sleep. Perhaps this was a sign of things to come.

In any case, all of the woodcuts in the book are black and white in the original. Considered along with the poems, they help to illuminate a journey, leaving you, the reader, to add colors of your own interpretation.

Prelude

Day and Night

We moved from the bright hub
of the suburb
to the quiet dark
of the woods
in search of the perfect life

Last night the moon
shone brightly over woods
illuminating the day
taking its turn with the sun
casting away shadows
of the night

Held by the moon of tradition
to expectations assigned
to each gender at birth
I move about tasks at home
to carry the generation forward

Powered by the sun of technology
current sweeps me forward
into a new frontier at work
teaching new roles
to inhabit and staff a changing world

I spend my days
in this cradling
between what was and what is
like in the cycle of day and night
from which there is no escaping

Gradually new roles shift life's base
and some begin to cut through life's river
like ice breakers in winter
opening a channel
through which the children can follow
into open waters
spring of their adulthood

The course is now set
for a new journey
there is no remaining
in an old world
melting into a new phase
not in the city
nor in the country

Contents

Perspective

Decision

Aspen leaves swivel in crisp wind
thoughts unable to rest.
Tree crowns dance endlessly.
I wait for time to pass.
Dusk slips into woods.
Through web of branches,
I strain to see sky's fading color
and the truth of my convictions
over and over again. A plane crosses above,
oblivious to life below. Where will my actions
take me, once I leave on a flight
uncharted and alone? The way up is steep
and far, like the dream to meet a friend
at the pyramids. Waiting beyond,
well within reach, mysterious and diverse,
forward moving, not planted, the city awaits.
From the open window I hear
faint sounds of birds, a dog barking,
wind stirring leaves—
a rhapsody of peacefulness.
Night descends, stills woods.
Windows move in black,
reflect lamps and a woman's image.

Catching Up

She was so far behind the rest,
she thought,
and hurried to catch up.
Though her efforts gained momentum,
the gap remained the same,
she thought.
For she did not know
that the impetus propelled her
beyond the point
which she conceived to be her goal,
that it would become the driving force
which conveyed her
to the land of the unknown,
to the realm of unfulfilled dreams,
that she might emerge from the depths
to expand and explore.

Momentum brought her
to the gates of a new land,
where she stood,
while surprise made her uncertain.
But she noticed a committee gathered
to welcome new arrivals,
handing out maps of a limited kind.
Wanderlust swelled in her veins,
and drew her to the outskirts of settlements,
to territories yet unknown.

And she started on the trek
winding into the future.
Somewhere in the distance,
she envisioned

open spaces to cross,
mountains to climb.
Inertia drove her forward now,
as she strained to gain speed again.
She was so far behind the rest,
she thought.

Realization

Rising River

Life's labyrinth
brought us to a river.

So I try harder
to go to school
   buy a new suit
to make it through the days.

By the lantern's light,
you stand, arms folded
   across chest,
patiently
   wanting to know:
"What is wrong?"
   Life left you
dissatisfied.

So the river keeps rising
over its banks
   threatening the house
near the shore.
   The lifeboat keeps us afloat.
We draw back midstream,
   follow the river's current,
careful to avoid traffic,
   floating debris.
We want to make it to the shore.
   But the shore moves inland
more each day.

Endless Sky

I

Pale sky is endless
above trees today.
Wilted oak leaves quiver
on branches in the cold.
Tree crowns stir gently,
rhythmically.
Here and there
squirrels scurry
along white ground,
select a tree,
nimbly rush up,
barely pause near branches
before leaping across
to another tree
as though borne on wings.
They land smoothly
or struggle to hang on
or balance precariously,
only to rush down again
to forage on the ground,
the way I have seen them do
countless times.

II

My parents owned a *Schrebergarten*
in Berlin, a few blocks distance
from the condominium where we lived
when I was ten. My older brother and I
often played there. It was our refuge
from city pavement and traffic,

a place where thoughts could touch
earth and sky, where imagination grew
like Vati's garden of vegetables,
red poppies and fruit trees
which he tended as though
they were artistic creations—or children.
I always avoided the small peach tree;
its fruit set my throat on fire.
But I liked the big cherry tree.

My brother and I would climb it eagerly
when cherries were ripe, too joyful
to bother with our usual squabbles.
In friendly competition we would collect
the abundant red treasures, cry out
ecstatically at clusters of cherries
which we showed off to each other,
draped over our ears like earrings. Then
we felt spurred to find more clusters
and picked and ate cherries, until
Dad said it was time to come down,
time to go home. Reluctantly,
we left our lofty paradise.

We would take home a basket of cherries
to share with the rest of the family.
Mom canned left-over cherries
in old bottles with wired caps
and stored them for winter. When she
brought out a bottle for dessert,
we watched the important event,
elbows on table, chins on hands.
Dad would empty the juice into a bowl,
then shake the upside-down bottle
reluctant to yield its luscious contents.

Sometimes, during hot summer days,
to keep us from the crippler disease,
in days before vaccinations,
Dad would pile my brother and me
into the old baby buggy, despite school,
and off to the garden we went,
delighted at the unexpected holiday.

My favorite spot in the garden
was the tool shed roof. I climbed it
to enter my private domain, away
from the bossy older brother,
and spent many hours surveying,
as from an ocean-going vessel.
Stretched out, I watched
formations of white clouds float across
summer blue sky, moving pictures
on a screen. Where were they going?
What sights would I see if I traveled
with them? How far to infinity?

III

Padded feet dash across
above my head.
I am glad for the music
of their company.
A squirrel's upside-down face
appears momentarily,
just below the overhang,
curiously peers
into my window,
then quickly
disappears while
I am recuperating from surgery.

From the bedroom window,
past the L-shaped edge
of the snow-covered roof,
I see through the web
of November trees,
a web too complicated
for me to want to untangle.
I focus instead
on the fading, endlessly blue
afternoon sky,
suspended.

IV

Dad will be eighty this November:
we had planned to take the kids
and drive the three hundred–plus miles
to Milwaukee, where he now tends
his garden of vegetables and flowers
and the fruit trees he recently planted,
as if to ensure creation everlasting.

At the edge
of the horizon,
a cloud
wraps itself—
a tattered,
purple-gray ribbon—
around the woods,
around the house
in its center.

Wings of Love

Love, as though touched by angel's wings,
casts its golden glow
over young lovers walking hand–in–hand
or newlyweds saying their vows,
or you and I dancing.
But the glow fades by and by,
as we walk the pavement of life.

Often, when I look for a token,
a sign from you,
it is like consulting the stars.
Then I wonder
if our love is gone.

Unfinished Project

I dreamt I walked
on a crowded beach.
People wore dark gray jackets
that cool, overcast day.

Gray waters swelled to the sky,
in the distance a boat.
Would it take me on board?

Just then, an older couple and a girl
examined the right front of a new coat
like one I remembered having begun
to construct some time ago.

"No," the girl said, "the coat
is too difficult to complete."
And her parents agreed. "Oh,"
she said, "but it has a good start."

She showed them, thus and thus,
how it could be done
and would make
an excellent coat in the end.

I felt what a pity
if the project were abandoned,
as I watched the boat
in the distance.

Reawakening

From the sun low in the diamond sky,
strands of early April gold
    streak the western side of the wood,
gild the earthen-colored forest floor,
    awaken the woods as from slumber.
Wind bristles rhythmically
    through dried oak leaves,
to the refrain of "Phoebe, phoebe,"
    ringing through the woods—
a crow calls somewhere in the distance.

The Rottweiler stays at my side now
while I rest, her face to the sun.
    Laying down, front paws stretched forward,
she sniffs the cool, dry air,
    watching the wood,
head erect, ears out at the sides.
    Soft brown eyes turn golden as she looks up at me
from time to time, while I stroke the black head
    with the mahogany spots dancing above the eyes—
a motor roars somewhere in the distance.

Rocks Do Not Think

I

Spring. At last,
Wisconsin's long winter
in the woods had passed.
The day was too nice to work inside.

The barberry bushes
looked like crows nests.
Trimming them, she felt a sting,
pulled out the thorn,
but the throb remained
as she continued her task.

The yard needed work,
before the jungle advanced,
swallowed it,
gradually taking over
plants and shrubs in its path,
cutting out the sun.

Sometimes she felt
she became part
of her surroundings,
submerged,
absorbed
by the lives of others,
absorbed
like water into a plant,
without substance of her own,
a fading shadow,
seeping into porous ground.

She wondered:
"Do I exist?"
Someone once said:
"I think. Therefore I am."

She added the new clippings
to the pile in the woods.
Insects swarmed in high humidity.
She waved them away.
Did insects think?

The large rocks between shrubs
looked pretty. Plentiful on their land,
they fit in well with smaller
landscaping rocks.
To give the shrub at the edge
more room, she stooped
to move the corner rock over—
without success.
She could not move it—or him.
It did not look that heavy—
Yet there it was—immovable.

She gathered flower pots,
emptied last year's soil,
washed the pots, when a hum
came closer. Had the water
attracted the bee?

Soup is a good meal for tonight,
she thought. They all like it.
Everything goes in one pot.

She stopped working for a moment,
inhaling springtime scents,

listening to bird voices.
With closed eyes,
she held on to the moment,
faced the sun,
felt the breeze on her skin,
wanting, craving more.

II

How do I know I really exist?
Is existence generic,
like soil or bee or soldier
or woman or ants
which were building a nest
under the deck?

What do I know of ants,
their society? Except they were
everywhere, gained entrance
into the house every summer,
despite attempts to control them,
tiny bodies working
for other tiny bodies.
She rinsed them away
with the garden hose,
conscious of the birds.

This summer she would fill
the space next to the deck
with potted impatiens.
Potted plants were not as likely
to be overrun by weeds
and brought color
to the wall of green.
Hummingbirds liked them.

What would we know of Caesar
had it not been for his conquests?
What of Brutus?
What would we know of Newton
had it not been for the apple?
What of gravitational forces?
What would we know of Emily Dickinson
had she not written poetry?

Her grandmothers?
She did not recall the sound
of their voices
nor had she read accounts
of their lives.
How do they live on in her?

Her grandfathers?
Mother's father was slight, ailing,
an upholsterer when he was young.
Dad resembled his father,
she recalled from a snapshot.
Dad said he had a great sense
of humor. When he was young,
Dad often accompanied grandfather
on business trip.

III

As she brought out more flower pots,
the robin suddenly darted out
of her nest with angry cries,
narrowly missing her, before landing
on the oak tree across.
"And I let you use our tree," she said.

"People are everywhere you go,"
he had said on a Sunday drive.
"Towns and cities are crowded;
suburbs are spilling over
into the country,
and you see houses on every hill,
at every turn."
Did he truly relish
a grassroots existence?

On the bottom of clean pots,
she placed small rocks,
walked to the toolshed
for the forty-quart bag of soil.
It weighed her down,
as though to sink her
below existence.

Sometimes life seemed to her
an inexhaustible debt:
the more you paid,
the more you owed;
the more you owed,
the more you submerged
until the flood waters
threatened to close in overhead.

She eased the bag down steps,
until it landed with a dull thud.
She pulled it behind her
across the lawn to the pots
which she filled with soil,
assembly-line style.

Her retired neighbors
down the road had moved away;
their name disappeared
from the mailbox one day.
They have a son out East,
she recalled.

Days later, she saw a van
in the driveway;
a man's name appeared
on the mailbox.
Was there also a Mrs.?
She went over
to welcome the new neighbors,
but no one answered the bell.

Then she got busy with kids and job.
Lining up plants, she thought,
someday soon,
she would like to meet them.

IV

She was planting
red and white impatiens,
when the school bus dropped off
the children. "You'll never believe
what happened today!" they cried
from the other end of the driveway.
"What happened?" she asked.
Rinsing soil off hands
with numbing water, she left things
where they were,

followed the children
into the house, wondering
if the robin had returned to the nest,
as they walked unmolested
past the evergreen.

Inside, they sat down
around the kitchen table,
ate crackers and cheese,
while she listenened and laughed
to enthusiastic reports of field day:
failures and fumbles,
efforts and triumphs.

The Agate

Among the rocks,
I found an agate
and I pondered:

If I dropped it
into a flower pot
along with other rocks,
covered it with soil,
would the agate still exist?

How will I remember
next year
where I put the pretty rock?

Visiting the Old Country

One year we traveled
from St. Paul to Düsseldorf,
first time ever,
he on business, I for company.

At the *Kaiserstraße*,
standing on the boulevard bridge,
I watched people go by,
people and sounds so familiar,
I expected Mom and Dad, arm in arm,
to round the corner at any time.

> "I will be in London for a day
> or two," he said.
> I dreaded spending the night alone
> so far from home.

> But in the evening,
> I walked through the *Altstadt*,
> window shopping, people watching
> on busy streets as though that was
> what I always did,
> and at the Heinrich Heine Stube
> dined on ragout with mashed
> potatoes and red cabbage,
> just like Mom used to make.

> The next morning
> I awakened to the music
> of childhood sounds, lost for so long.
> I came back to myself unexpectedly,
> spring into river.

Outside people and traffic rushed
to the streetcar's hum and "bim bim,"
sounds I recalled
from my grandparents' house
in the Berlin of my childhood.

Forearms on window sill,
I leaned out the hotel window,
the way people did in the old country
on balmy summer nights,
the way neighbors sit
on front steps in the Midwest.

Children carrying school bags passed,
and I remembered my first painstaking attempts
at making letters in first grade.
Women passed carrying shopping bags,
like the one Mom once used for groceries.

The gap between childhood
and adulthood closed,
when a television program
interviewed people on the state
of their country, sending my thoughts
to circle years and worlds to add
the outsider's view from the inside out.

I looked and spoke like them,
moved around much like one of them.
They did not notice that I am
an American from the Midwest,
until I told them so.

The second half of the twentieth century
had arrived here

just as it had in America,
with push-button conveniences,
fast food restaurants, and traffic jams.

They all belonged to me, that time.
I was "home," away from home, alone
for the very first time—

I carried back the childhood connection
to my parents, who do not remember
things that way in this blending of times
and worlds. They continue family traditions,
home in Milwaukee, where they help color
the lives of their grandchildren now.

Going from here to the Old World
was much like stepping
from living room to dining room
of the same house,
a house located in the New World.

Changing Current

The Navigator

She took a sailboat out to sea
To sail the sea of life –
The mighty sea then heaved and roared
At such a fool that be
And turned the sailboat upside down
To show its great contempt –
Expelling water, stretching forward
She strained against its might –
In numbing waters, deep and gray –
To swim to safety's sandy shore –

The surging waves of time –
Like rising mountains rolled at sea –
And plunging toward shore
Their white heads crashed on rocks –
Waves grasped the swimmer in the sea
Like deadwood floating free –
Yet helpless to protest –
The murky waters thus conveyed
And swept her to the rocky beach
As though they were in jest –

But mind, unbroken,
Took the body into tow.
With worthier vessel, then –
The sea once more she sailed.

Summer Evening

Alone
on a warm, sweet scented
summer evening.
Woods sound a symphony
of bird voices,
rose-breasted grosbeak,
chickadees
and nuthatches,
woodpecker's drill,
cardinal's flourish,
flurry of birds passing
between trees and feeders.
Dusk descends;
voices fade.
The butterfly
seeks its home
for the night.
Potted impatiens
surround me
on the deck.
The dog sleeps
curled up
at my feet.
A last chirp
here and there,
then calm,
peace.
A letter came.

Tornado Country

Tornado country this –
Not to be fooled
by sunshine
or calm
when thunder rumbles
in the distance –
Life goes on as usual
between storms
Most times the funnel
only sweeps by
the sound of a train
or explosion
when it strikes
splattering a lifetime –
Rebuilding is slow
love becomes
mother to apprehension –
It could happen again –
It is only a question
of time

The Woman and the Mountain

The woman climbing the mountain
on her lone trek
felt like the man
on Mt. St. Helens
who had lived there
all his married life
in the house where
his spouse died.
He could not leave
the memories
when the volcano erupted.

Earthbound

Pink clouds cross the evening sky
in unending array of tufts
like thoughts that take shape,
reshape as currents direct,
grow into larger patterns and forms.

Earthbound we watch,
recede into dusk;
darkness holds us spellbound
not wanting us to know secrets
clouds bear into the distance.

Great Lake

I

Bathers crowd on the hot, sandy beach,
    storehouse
    of sunshine and romance,
seek summer's reprieve,
    ride waves
    in water that numbs limbs.
Endlessly, crested waves surge forward, pound
    shoreline rocks
    in a lullaby of fallen kings.
Sailboards glide north, dip forward,
    flutter in waves
    like colorful butterflies.
In the distance, sailboats cross
    in midday haze
    like scale models,
respectfully clear a freighter at anchor.
    Blue-green
    Lake Michigan curves
into faded canvas dome sky.
    Swallows scan
    water's surface.
Seagulls patrol gates of the Great Lake's
    chilly domain.

II

Along the breakwater, open shirt inflates
    like the sail of a ship.
Damp air tastes of fish.

A fisherman explains to a woman
    how to reel in
    her line.
Hair flies from face; wind wraps head,
    soothes body,
    whistles softly.
Small fish lies motionless, forgotten
    on breakwater block.
    Fishermen cast lures.
Minnows swim frantically in jars, pails,
    await their
    inevitable fate.

III

Beyond bars, the sign reads "Danger.
    Keep out."
    Large cement blocks
piled side by side, stretch east.
    Empty bottles, cans
    lodge in crevices here and there.
With foaming fists the Great Lake pounds blocks,
    reaches cold fingers
    over sandaled feet,
rising to draw onlookers into his depths.
    To the west, dark
    massive buildings
tower, confront. Flat-faced and
    hollow-eyed,
    they stare back at
the mighty sea god in his preserve.

Without Vision

What is this weight draped over me?
What arms hold,
    leave me leaden, hazy,
without vision for tomorrow?

    The house stands
surrounded by forest,
    amidst chickadees, nuthatches,
free roaming deer.

    It stands, as if sprawling hope
on ground too solid for light steps
    which echo in dark hallways,
where speech and laughter distort,
    and words become trapped behind closed doors.
Delicate treasure of the past, they
    remain locked in a windowless room.

    Each year trees lean
over the house more,
    as though wanting to comfort
but crowding instead.

    Days pass behind a glass bowl
while the metropolis across the river awaits,
    inaccessible in the distance over icy roads,
beckoning with the hub of familiar voices.

Summer's End

I

Summer's green is transforming
into yellow, gold, and rust.
Bird houses are vacant.
Flocks of birds gather in the sky.
After summer's flurry and frenzy,
quiet descends like a spell
over western Wisconsin's woods.
Chickadees and nuthatches
take turns dashing
between feeder and bird bath;
their voices ring like faint chimes.
Hummingbirds sip nectar
to a propeller-like hum.
Blue jays pierce the air
with distant cries.
Sun rays gently embrace woods
in summer's good-bye.

II

Years seep into ground
having nourished children
now grown up.
They scatter into the world
of school and work
like fledgelings trying wings.
A son returns home from school
for a week-end visit,
more self-confident and manly
than before. He smiles

at his mother across the table
over a home-cooked meal.
A daughter rushes in and out
on her way to work,
to meet friends,
to find an apartment of her own.
She stops long enough
to nourish
the adult friendship with parents.

III

After the children leave,
the house seems larger, darker
than before, echoing only
what used to be,
in the fading days of summer.

Beneath a Sickle Moon

Beneath stars and sickle moon
wind rustles through oak woods,
thick with darkness, pierced
by faint, persistent chirps.

I

Nights of giving birth,
days of bringing infants home
seem only a yesterday away.
Today children tower
like young trees
above their mother,
who once nourished them
with her milk.
They now dwarf her
with youthful resolve
and the knowledge
the world is theirs.
They forge ahead,
trade children's songs
for on-stage performance,
plastic models
for refurbished cars.
Children become stars
to whom the mother looks up.

II

The mother's days become empty,
fill with thoughts
of what was and might be
and her need to create and do
while he is at work till late every day.
There has to be more.
"You are crazy," he said.
"The house will keep you busy."
And she keeps house, as usual
eating dinner alone,
plants new seeds in the garden,
tailors new suits in her workroom,
joins a club in town,
volunteers at school.
Still, she senses,
there has to be more,
senses a need to be needed,
to give birth to a child
of another dimension.

    Dawn slowly splatters gray
    through tree tops. Near
    the kitchen window, the owl hoots
    as though bidding good-bye
    to its friend, the waning night.

Fall

In open fields,
large flocks of birds
gather
to fly south

A hush has fallen
over the woods.
Bare trees sway in wind,
exposing empty nests.

Quiet has descended
over the neighborhood, too,
with children
back to school.

The house now visible
from the road
stands quiet,
the children back in college.

The dog comes to my side,
and I am left to ponder
my purpose,
my own empty nest.

October Woods

Against white-tufted sky, woods bloom
    aspen green, birch gold,
white oak rust—sun-fired.
    Beneath dry oak leaves,
pink and red impatiens,
    having outlasted summer,
look discordant and wilting.
    Summer's barren rosebush
greets October sun
    with the year's solitary blossom—
red, sweet-scented.
    Exposed, the grand house
of rough cedar and brick
    nestles among leaves
as though seeking cover.
    Deer cross the road,
past No Hunting or Trespassing signs,
    yet watchful of the glassy-eyed house,
behind which they amble
    down the path into the valley below.
Autumn's hush, moist, warm air
    prepare the forest
for winter's long sleep.

Shaking tails like banners,
    two squirrels face each other
on opposite sides of an oak,
    racing on track.
Chickadees take over the feeder again,
    while nuthatches drop down
intermittently. Seasonal change lures
    some birds to new territory.

Woods-mirrored window panes claim
    those leaving feather tufts
like calling cards.
    One nuthatch lies on a bed of leaves,
feet pointed heavenward; next to it,
    another sits, appearing asleep
and strangely tame,
    on a journey abruptly halted.
Slowly, it opens its eyes,
    body trembling, drunk with pain.
Slowly, wings strain, awkwardly,
    propel it aloft.
The oak tree takes the nuthatch
    into its rust-colored harbor.
Tree crowns rock gently,
    in rhythm to autumn winds.

Going West

Time and torrents washed out
old roads
though remnants still remain.
Looking for pieces of asphalt
of the once solid road
in the valley below
may risk a mudslide in descent.

A new generation,
I follow the sunset
without signs or paved roads,
not knowing what lies ahead,
a pioneer searching for new land
but concerned
I may encounter ghost towns;
a prospector looking for gold
but realizing
I could be waylaid;
a dreamer wondering
if Canada's winds will wake me.

Blue skies beckon me on
to cross plains,
dare me forget about badlands,
urge me to climb Rockies, to glimpse ahead
in search of the future.

Autumn Rain

In the distance
gray sky meets charcoal road.
Open space fills with rain
like a doorway hung with beads.

Rain soaks autumn's earth,
nourishes, protects
before winter.

Rain pours itself out
unashamed of its mission,
the way words pour out of a pen,
words that flow unimpeded.

Quest

Quest

Thoughts cruise low
like swallows
on a humid summer day.

On the morning of my move
in dim light, the air hangs heavy
over the dark, massive house.

Hopeful for the future,
sad for the departure
and no one to say good-bye to,
except years of a task fulfilled,
I leave the forest.

Gaining energy
with the advancing day,
I cross the river bedded in fog.

Gulls circle high, fall back,
like thoughts
not yet ready to fly between states.

The Pulse

Every night
I have dinner in my apartment
as if at the top
of the Radisson, where
the platform turns with diners
overlooking the city.
Arteries pulse below;
lights flow like blood cells,
moving traffic on roads
above and below
and at right angles.
Red and green lights gleam,
scatter darkness,
reining in and releasing
energy bursts.

Reflecting
on my past
wooded existence
in this halfway road motel,
I hold the scene below
like a framed picture.
The building across
blocks the view,
as though to obscure
what lies ahead.
Still, this is a starry night,
and past my window,
roads lead to the city's heart.

Sentinels of the Forest

I have returned,
a pilgrim,
to December Oaks,
sentinels, watching over forest life,
to meditate over what remains
and where life may lead.

Oak woods so open,
after fall's brief glory,
reveal traces of life,
hide little from observer's eye now,
not the empty wren house,
nor the squirrel's nest.

What silent witness have they been
to our lives
to people passing,
from days when Indians
inhabited the land?

What silent witness have they been
to scarlet tanager
playing catch one distant spring
when people felled his trees
to make room for their house?

Oaks filled out each summer,
leaned into the clearing,
over the house,
as if to reclaim more space
year by year,
oaks alive with bird voices,
a wall of green.

Unaffected by warm November days,
oaks mock plants that nudge heads
through earth, expecting spring.
Oaks are ready to resist winter's blade,
accept its snowy blanket
over straight or knotty growth.

Holding dormant vigil,
December oaks prophesy nothing,
disclose only that which
the eye is ready to see.
Yet their promise of another spring
nourishes my soul.

Home for Christmas

I. Preparation

To go home again—because I promised—
like every year.
But only Angie and I, this time.
Her brother Bill will meet us there.
We watch the weather
as if it were life's unpredictable spirit
hovering over the day-long trip.

II. Pilgrimage

Parents await us, a welcoming committee
at the door. Other family members have
already arrived. We reenter the family sphere
with embraces and gifts, dinner waiting
and dad pacing excitedly after the hellos.

Mom gathers the family around the table,
festively laid out, serves the dinner
Father prepared. With the passing
of food, we reconnect, discovering pieces
of the family puzzle. We find our parents'
features randomly distributed among children
and grandchildren, eyes and hair color, chins,
and voices, hands and movements
in a reassembly of genes. We pass the roast
and gravy, Dad's gourmet experiment,
over questions of brother Frank's job,
pass potatoes and vegetables over the outcome
of a niece's tonsilectomy. Mom encourages
seconds, and we toast across the table,

crystal glasses ringing out. Silently we sip
homemade wine, smiling at each other
over the rim of wine glasses. Mom winks
at Dad across the table, as if they shared
a carefully guarded secret, woven
into their union of over fifty years.
He smiles back, and we fill our plates
a second time but mindful to save room
for Mom's *Apfelkuchen*. Mom serves
Dad first, then the anxiously waiting
grandchildren, and finally us. Angie and I
exchange smiles, while she serves
her little cousin a second helping of desert.
The child's eyes sparkle mischievously,
having claimed her father's lap for herself.
Another niece comes to cuddle at my side,
as we finish the meal, discussing
the connection between human spirit,
religion, and the arts, ending in Dad telling
his favorite joke that results in smiles
and Bill responding, "Oh, Grandpa!"

We move to the joyful chaos of opening gifts,
followed by countless hugs and thank yous
and excited outcries of children
in their treasure hunts. Late in the evening,
those living in town, say their good-byes.

We are glad our visit has only begun.
The next few days our lives interweave
with my parents' lives. They pamper us
with hearty meals and reminders
to dress warmly. Mom shows off
her new suit, consults me about which shoes
match best. We go shopping, she and I

advising each other as to what looks
and fits best. Father is pleased,
at least part of the family is together,
bringing excitement into their days.
While they rest, I write, and Dad
says: "Good, you are working. It's
just like the old days." I smile,
simultaneously transposed back in time
but absorbing the present moment
that seeks to make up and compress
months of separation into a few days'
visit. Days later, we treat them to dinner
at Dietze's Restaurant and treasure
last hours before returning home.

III. Promise

Leaving early in the morning, we hurry
home on dry, sunlit roads. Traveling,
I imagine the future, new beginnings
beyond the next turn, when I note a figure
move across the road in the distance,
only to see a road sign emerging
as we round the curve. How deceiving,
limited, perspective can be, like the turn
of a relationship so right at the outset,
moving apart, in time,
despite efforts to continue,
or attempts to work out differences.
So we traveled roads paved and repaved
and reconstructed many times.

Content with our progress, we enjoy dinner
at a lively restaurant, while skies cloud over,
leaving us to navigate ice-glazed roads,
when we continue our journey. Behind us,
the truck follows too closely for conditions.

We note cars nesting in snow-packed ditches
and people wading in ankle-deep snow.
Early evening suddenly turns midnight.
Driving becomes a procession.

How things change so unexpectedly,
from child's dream to woman's reality.
Two roads to travel—
one, mother's direction, to put husband first—
the other, father's dream to be anything I want to be—
in an age changing so quickly.
Two roads built into one dream.
Where did I miss the signs, let the dream
gradually blur, steeped in the importance
of nurturing, caring, tending children, husband,
and household?   Still, with the children grown up,
there is room, room for more. Life is change,
continuous as the road, like Dad taking over
the cooking after we had left. Life is growth,
like Mom pursuing knitting and embroidery
and above all, her reading, now that she
doesn't have to prepare all the meals. If only
my husband could understand that living
and adapting, moving forward to the drum
of a new movement, the speed of technology,
is not for industry and business alone.

IV. Direction

The truck behind us does not see the need
to leave more space between us. The car
in front of us dictates the speed. I sense
danger, wedged in between the two. Gently,
I ease the car into the passing lane. Gradually,
I accelerate, leaving car and truck—
and a long line of cars—behind.

Silence

Last night I dreamt he came
to see me, smiling
his impenetrable smile.
Broad shouldered,
he wore business gray
with wide lapels,
double-breasted
and immaculately fitted.

Not one word passed
between us. But, oh –
how I would have liked to plead.

The House

In the dream
the house was on fire.
Seeking a way out,
I found windows shuttered,
front door sealed.
I lifted the telephone receiver,
while flames licked the ceiling.
The voice on the other end
blurred; then the line went dead.

    The woman on screen
    sits in front
    of the charred shell
    of her house,
    holding her baby.
    "We lost everything,"
    she says, leaning her head
    against her baby's. "But
    we are lucky: We are all right."

Inside the home built
over a dream, we lived
in separate rooms
of our being, until the dream
ran out. The children saw
it coming from a distance,
the smoke ring
through which we slipped,
first he, then I. We left behind
the house and moved on
in separate directions.

Mourning

She left him
as surely
as he left her.

She did not know when
they first began to change
directions. She only knew
the candle in his eyes
had burned out.

No love letters had ever passed
between them. They each spoke
a dialect of their own, until
they were certain they had found
a common language.

Summers they spent
at the beach with their children.
Winters they went dancing
with friends, until she noticed
him slipping through the circle.

Feelings either seeped
into the ground
or were shut away in a safe.

For they lived in the real world
of big houses and beautiful people,
world travelers of the industrial age,
where winning was the only game
and giving was rent due.
In the end, they both lost
view of what really mattered.

In sleepless nights, she looked
at the moon, while he slept
through dreamless hours.

Seeking light, she looked
for answers. She wanted
to plant the rose
he once mowed even with the lawn
into new soil.

Hope

Red-winged blackbird,
bird of open spaces,
soft, familiar song
awakens me this morning.

At the window I see only
crows rakishly ascend
above buildings, their calls
cutting through city sounds.

Cars and trucks pass,
carry commuters and loads,
into distance and obscurity
as if to disappear, forever.

Across, holiday inn thoughts
attempt to vacation, turn
inward to the dawn, raise a flag
beneath the sunlit sky.

Empty Beach

From the dead-end street
of my existence,
I crossed the river,
to hope's other shore.

    When I was a child,
    I liked to explore
    the world around me.
    When I was at summer camp
    at the beach one day,
    thunder clouds swept over the sun
    while kids swam and played.
    Counselors signaled children
    to leave the water, then,
    and to return to camp.

With excited screams
and splashes, they all headed
for the beach,
as if for some grand event.

    Straggling behind,
    I found the lake,
    calm and peaceful,
    without people pushing
    or splashing—
    so I stayed behind to frolic
    in open and inviting water.

    Current pulled—
    I followed,
    just to see how far

I could go,
ballerina on toes.
Chin deep I swayed
in Neptune's powerful arms,
that carried me deeper
and deeper
into the watery kingdom.

Submerged
and unable to swim,
I flailed in suffocating darkness,
breathing fire.
Then toes touched sand.
Pushing off, I emerged a whale.
When feet grasped bottom again,
toes dug in, strained
toward shallower water —
willowy legs carried,
beached their load
on warm sand.

Lightning split slate sky;
thunder followed a whip lash.
On the gray, empty beach,
my anchored body seemed
to stretch to infinity.

It was then
I began to tremble
on the deserted beach,
cold rain drops on my skin.

What will it be like when,
for the first time,
I start life on my own, moving
into an uncharted future?

Beyond Sunset

Looking for the movie theater,
someone points: "There!"
and we watch

three geese flying low,
kite formation,
beneath gray-streaked sky.

Long necks stretch,
like life moving forward,
into the sunset.

Each year,
they reach
spring's habitation.

Each year
they persist, oblivious to smog,
foul water, or hunting season.

They arrive,
without hesitation,
knowing, without comprehending—

Distracted,
we speed past our destination,
unknowing, yet wanting to discover—

Uncharted Passage

Parting

Stoutly, he stands next to the truck
in the apartment parking lot.
He smiles as I accept his help,
wondering why it came so easily.

He stands before me, familiar, solid,
in business gray and bold striped tie
I helped him select. I hesitate,
wearing jeans and white shirt,
wondering why I am so blasé.

For the first time, he agrees that I
made the right decision. Like old friends,
we consider our lives then and now.
Like brokers, we examine our individual
futures, changing markets,
risks, and romantic prospects,
but without the usual tension.

He notes how much more at ease I am
now. Having both changed, we would
surely get along. I look neither right
nor left, just straight ahead, the way
I have countless times before,
lest a wrong move set off the pain,
lest it draw me into the vacuum again.

The invitation to come in, like
the way back, is but a door away.
A door he cannot open without my key.
Yet my hand does not reach for the door,
shut so many times by the draft

of voiced and unvoiced conflict.
Instead, the impulse slips away. I
wish it would not have to be this way.
He climbs into his truck; I hurry upstairs.
He waves from behind the wheel
of his car; I wave back from behind
glass doors, remembering times when
our parting was no casual feat.

Haunted

From sunny road
I turn into the driveway cut into oak woods.
Shrubbery and trees intimately surround
sprawling, stone-faced house,
built on former Indian land,
in contest between people and forest.
I enter and cool, damp darkness
    takes me back.

The dog comes,
bone in mouth, sits in front of me, and I
pet the warm black head. When I let
her out, she explodes with energy,
running in circles aound the lawn,
with occasional leaps
    in my direction.

Hummingbirds look in vain
for flowers this year and hover
in front of large window panes that reflect
woods. I walk into spacious, partly disassembled
rooms, as though visiting a dream, where
I find things lacking the brightness
I remember; dried roses remind me
of faded love; pictures replaced by posters,
    become page marks of life's transience.

Outside, oaks stand their ground,
like undefeated spirits of another time,
crowns cut by window frames. The mind's palm
wants to go out raised to stop their steady
advance. Inside, the ficus tree,
whose dry leaves litter the floor, seeks light.
    I take two cuttings.

Lyrics of "Bridge
Over Troubled Water" reverberate in memory
of years past, cradled in tree crowns,
while squirrels leap from tree to tree,
as though anxiously seeking answers
    in their daily acrobatics.

    Numb, I pry myself away,
as if in a trance. As though
on an every-day errand, I leave.
Crossing aquamarine waters of the river,
I wonder what I feel: no gloom or sadness,
this time, just a lightening of shoulders.
I gun the car, glide across the border
like a sailboat, glad for the clear day,
    hair blowing in the wind.

Walk Through Battle Creek Park

You enter, lively like the creek,
whose waters rush and tumble
over the dam into the lagoon
in July's drought—

And we walk best friends,
side by side in the park.
I feel your energy renew mine,
while your stream of words slows
to a constant, steady flow.

Amid water lilies and reeds,
a mother duck watches her
ducklings wade in the shallows
of the lagoon's receding waters.

We are pleased: At least for now,
life's continuity is assured.
And you confide beginnings
of your new romance to me.

Crunching across stubby, dry grass,
no longer inviting for picnic or
relaxation, you point out a maple
wilting from blight and lack of rain.

We pass the busy playground
that was a meadow
when you were small.
I recall the lively toddlers who kept
me running, while watching them play.

You tell me about college classes.
I remind you to balance class load
with life's other essentials.

Hesitating at the trail's fork,
we quibble, each wanting the other
to choose, until passers-by chuckle.
We follow the trail marked "Bicycles"
on one side, "Pedestrians" on the other.

We cross the road to the woods
that used to be part of an old farm
considered by city fathers,
at one time, as site for a future zoo.

I ponder my uprooted life alone:
Will I ever derive order out of chaos?
You are convinced I will.

We discover two ponds, well hidden
from street and casual observer.
You run up a side path to explore.
Wearing flimsy sandals, I wait
the way I did when you were small.

Blackberry bushes along the trail
are heavy with immature berries,
and we promise each other
to return when they are ripe.

The park extends to the road
and the mysterious parking lot
we see driving by. We had the best
of country and city right here
all along and did not even know it.

At the next fork, the path leads back
to the road instead of on through
the park. To escape traffic, we find
a shortcut across the old sports field
and head back through the woods,

confident to find a path, however small.
The park has become a labyrinth,
like our lives. You follow me, as we
trudge through thicket and high grass.

Hands pass branches, like thoughts,
as we warn each other of difficult
footing. My pace slows when sandals
entangle in brush. Now you
take the lead, secure in hiking boots,
when you spot the meadow ahead.

Thankful for the constants in life,
we laugh, having arrived together,
too, at a new direction,
mother and daughter,
both striking out on their own.

That evening, feeling renewed
and eager to go on to other things,
you return for yet another hug,
then rush off, speed past my balcony,

sun-streaked, in the green Rebel,
strawberry blonde hair blowing
streamers out the car window,
arm waving as though you had just
crossed the finish line—Angelica!

The Meeting

We met
in the waiting room, greeted each other
smiling, not like lovers or spouses but
like business associates. Clutching briefcase,
he confided uneasiness; I confessed
a similar state. He deplored high fees
of lawyers, who kept us waiting as though
our time were theirs. I agreed.

We sat across
from each other in the conference room,
not side by side, cast quick glances
at one another, not to flirt or support,
but to detect. We divided past and future
as if they were mathematical equations.
And when what was ours became his and mine,
he slumped into his chair. I felt remorse,
then removed, a bystander, unable to speak,
staring blankly past him, out the window.
He accepted the lawyer's remarks without
rebuttal, sending glances, instead of words,
in my direction. "You have rights, too,"
the lawyer said to me privately later on.

I left, wondering
when love first became incidental, gradually
petrified into habit or routine, when kisses
became the familiar, embraces the expected,
and smiles a substitute for contentment.
It must have happened unnoticed, little by
little over the years the way one becomes
accustomed to living in a damp, dark house

until one no longer notices. In the end,
we were left with a residue of rights and
regrets, pain, and anguish. What are rights
in the face of love?

That night, rain
pelted parched land. Thunder rumbled
through restless sleep. Words of a sermon
echoed in my mind: "There is no quick fix."
So let it pass. Let it pass—

Summer Web

Sunbeams web
over land and people. Air too heavy
to breathe drains the body of energy.

When, at last, rain
sweeps in, it runs off hardened earth.
Wind scatters raindrops that vanish
in cracks. Rain runs off soil to feed rivers
or turns into puddles on pavement.

Each year we wait
for summer behind closed windows,
recall how good summer used to feel,
how sun and rain turned the outdoors green,
plants and trees now wilting yellow and brown.

We feel misplaced
in a dreamscape, as greenhouse turns
northern desert, and small Minnesota lakes
and ponds transform into valleys of death.

What devotion can
compensate for such extremes? Helplessly,
we watch water and birds recede more,
while the web tightens anew
by the week, the month.

Changed ozonosphere,
sends relentless gleam. Atmosphere,
like an overheavy hand on the shoulder,
numbs limb and imagination,
leaves birds struggling for survival.

Steady hum of air conditioner
saturates the room. And for those who
have not yet learned how to pray,
body and mind become separate
travelers, heartening each other on
through this valley. The web holds.

All that remains is the wait.

Treasure Hunt

Inside the fortress of woods
the house sprawls downhill.
The foyer receives me
with arms of darkness.
Like a stranger,
I hold back keys that seek
their accustomed tray.

Downstairs,
the sewing room opens into light.
Last year's fashion pictures
stare back outdated from walls
with the look that once
was so right.

The three-way mirror
holds my reflection. I remember,
one day, when fitting a suit, I briefly
caught my father's probing glance looking
back at me, as if looking for perspective
in his picture, startling me
to realize the connection.

Closet shelves loom oppressively
with piles of old fabrics and remnants,
like old, neglected memories,
needing to be sorted,
like souls awaiting disposition,
each wanting to be brought out,
touched, smoothed, saved.

Scraps of children's shirts and pants,
of an old coat donated to Goodwill, long ago,
cottons, wools, synthetics, fabrics
for every weather and occasion
of half-forgotten days
pass through my hands.

Accustomed in the past
to waste nothing,
induced by diligence
to treasure all,
I hold close for just a moment
these transient images of life's flow,
of my children growing
through colorful swatches,
page markers of life's progression,
of occasions and events.

"Just think how much money
you saved sewing," Billy says,
his smile brightening his face.
"He is just like you," Dad had said
the other day.

"But wait!"
Billy's fingers run across metallic silver
fabric, fake fur, and black velvet,
his blue eyes deepening.
His left hand submerged
in mounds of multicolored fabrics,
he says: "Perhaps I can use
some of these." Holding up pieces
of fabric, he visualizes aloud the effect
on the old model car he is about
to refurbish to create the wheeled future
he cannot yet afford.

Surprised at the extent
of his creativity,
I am glad some of the pieces
have found a new home.

His father enters smiling
to receive requested pieces
of old sheeting
for cleaning windows.

Darkness falls
as I lose myself
in multicolor terry print
that could grace a picnic table
or wrap a body after bath,
lose myself
in the gray wool
that would make a new skirt
for a still-wearable suit jacket
whose skirt no longer fits.
I put them in a box,
creating a bond between
past and future.

Content with his find,
Billy pushes bulging bags
of old remnants beneath the now empty
shelves and helps me carry out
two boxes of salvaged fabric, like children
who come along on the journey.

Outside,
on our way to the car,
beneath shadows of advancing night,
fireflies as never before,
stop us in awe
with their Fourth of July fireworks.

Interval

Into the shadow,
with long swinging legs,
I walk the path made
for hikers and lovers.

Through crunch and swirl
of October leaves,
I walk past empty playground
and empty picnic tables.
Brisk wind fingers my hair
like a playful spirit
remindful of the changed season.

Bedded between newly-green meadow,
the lagoon once more teems with birds
all full-grown now. The lagoon's waters
are replenished, as though summer's drought
never was. The new season draws fresh
energy for fall's journey south. Mallards
dip into water, small against Canada geese
that glide on its surface. In pairs
or formation geese rise, draw banners
across the sky, then descend, majestically,
at the lagoon's other end in a drill
of upcoming migration. A woman,
dispensing bread into the air
lures sea gulls who gather and scatter
on the meadow. A lone crow calls,
escaping to the edge of the woods—

Not ready for fall,
I have lost
the accustomed wish
to move on to some other

inviting place this year.
So I linger a while longer—

Then, slowly, zipping jacket
against the wind, I walk
from shadow into burst
of warm evening sun.

Restless

Thoughts flutter
   here and there
like birds seeking seeds
   before the storm.

Is it you I miss,
   solitude I seek?
a place to belong?

Last night, your voice
   so familiar
over the phone,
   sounded like home.

I strained to see,
   but the image faded
into darkness.

And the words
   that call home
never crossed
   the lips.

Crossing the Bridge

We sit and wait,
as on a train
moving too fast
to stop now.

Landscape flits past
in scenery of our lives.
He spent his days
directing people
to move upward
build better machines,
increase profit.
Nights and weekends,
he cleared trees
layed concrete foundation
on which we built
what became a wooden dream.

I held the ladder,
cooked meals,
made his dream a home
by day. I chauffered children
to sports events and music lessons,
to Cub Scouts and Girl Scouts,
invited the neighbors at Christmas.
At night,
I pondered over bills,
rocked children
to the stars,
until they were on their own.
Years of making do,
working hard and saving
pass like billboards—
and the destination so near.

He traveled in tracks
of facts and equations.
I grew in space of sewing
dreams into pyramids.

Two parallel lines
do not intersect.
And space opens
as children grow up.

We sit waiting,
speeding toward
a black tunnel.
We study the future
already embedded in seams
of marble slabs
on the salt-and-pepper
courthouse floor.

In the conference room,
we sit side by side,
the lawyers opposite
each other, like opponents.

Left alone,
we argue.
In the bare,
pictureless room,
imagination is trapped,
and I hesitate,
then leave the room,
suddenly unafraid.

At last,
we seal final agreement
with a cigarette
which burns down
in my hand unsmoked.
Quickly, counsel prods me
to a neutral corner.

We are gathered here today
behind double doors,
performers and spectators,
to collect the scores
of legal guidelines
and shuffleboard.

Having begun the day
as if preparing
for surgery,
we enter the room beyond,
stepping on stage.

Observation theater
stands empty today.
Pulse is taken.
We rehearse once more.

Then anesthetic takes hold.
I feel my body rise.
My eyes turn crystal and sting.

Legalities round
between judge,
who nods kindly to us,
and lawyers,
who know the answers.

Words labor across my lips,
"yes" and "no"
and "I think so."
We both understand the law.

No recovery room here,
no relatives or friends.
I hesitate and float
through doors and hallways,
uncertain of my direction,
turning on my heel.
"No one wins here," his
lawyer says behind me.

On the street I stand,
knowing he
is still upstairs.

From across the street,
he no longer looks
so commanding,
only solid, as always,
and in need of support.

White temples frame dark,
pained eyes that used to be
bright crystal green,
hands clutching briefcase.

"Let's stay friends,"
he echoes my words
of one year ago,
and we shake hands.
He solicits a kiss
which I place on his cheek.

We wave goodbye,
clearing snow from windshields,
drive off
in different directions.

As if on automatic pilot,
I cross the snowy bridge.
On the other side,
cars are strewn every which way.

The opposite lane, blocked
by a jack-knifed semitrailer,
lines up two lanes of cars,
lights beaming to the sky.

I face the storm's
white tongue,
holding merely a name,
knowing only
I have entered the new season.

And city lights
are waiting ahead.

Looking for Signs

Thanksgiving

Jupiter
brightest among stars
of the declining year
supreme among old gods
holds our attention tonight

Two children home
for Thanksgiving break
visit
They talk
of school and friends
lively and eager
Their eyes explore
the kitchen time and again
for clues
of the home-cooked meal

At last we pass turkey
mashed potatoes and gravy
for a second time
make crystal glasses ring out
in our communion
renewing ties
that free

Then on the balcony
they point out Jupiter
in the eastern sky
Jupiter
candle on the altar
of our Hope
prompts us

to gauge position
measure progress
in the vastness
of our new world
On separate journeys
just begun
we are navigators
each of our own dream
and we hold Promise
in its light

Jupiter
constant
timeless
tonight, we follow His sign

Let It Snow

On the first day
of Advent
snow gently
covers gray ground
to purify
and make its bed
preparing for rebirth
Snow swirls down
from rooftops
fresh against the cheek
making us breathless
And we laugh softly
as we hurry
into the sanctuary

Let it snow

Minnesota Winds

Lash sheets of snow
over land and city
suffocating March
until the eyes hurt
howling the relentless
seasonal refrain

Those trapped
by snow warnings
watch
from behind window panes
relieved food is stocked
counting days to spring

Only the spirited dare
hold out a gloved palm
admire snow flakes
make snow angels
ski across fresh country
wind pinching cold
damp cheeks

Sunrise
and the world has tunneled
out of the new layer
pulse quickens
with its ascent
signaling
hibernation's end

Garden on KK River Parkway

Headwaters

Doors and windows are open, as usual,
my parents' house ready to receive
children and grandchildren
visiting headwaters of their river.

Today, Dad shows us the garden.
Mom's Mona Lisa-like smile
never leaves her face,
as if the plants and flowers,
shrubs and trees were their
intimate secret, revealed to us
for the very first time.

The Garden

Like Moses in the Promised Land,
Dad leads us on a tour through his
garden, the way he does almost
every year, green eyes scrutinizing,
his tall figure slightly hunched,
like when he works on a sketch
taped to the wall—the garden,
informal and seemingly boundless,
the raw material of creation.

The newly planted vine
on the east side of the house
will cover the brick wall
and cool it on hot summer days.

We will soon eat freshly picked
lettuce and tomatoes, he says.
Potted strawberry plants
are in full bloom.

Lilies of the valley,
which once came from my garden,
shoots of plants Dad had
originally given me, are spreading.
French lilacs thrive. He will have
a shoot for me, when I am ready.

He moves among apple, plum,
and pear trees. He planted them
during his three-quarter-century spring
of living. He studies trees,
as if he were preparing to sketch them.
His arms swoop down to show how
they will droop fruit-laden at harvest.
He heralds the first two cherries
of a two-year-old tree, pausing, sighing
as if he were watching children grow.

Fired up by his energy,
Angie eagerly offers to return to help
at harvest time. Her grandmother's
smile broadens at the prospect.

"It's all in the cow manure,"
Wolfgang chuckles, pointing
to the fruit trees like to pictures
in an art exhibit. When the neighbor
asks about the strong odor,
whose origin he cannot place,
Wolfgang says with a laugh: "Why,

I tell him: That's good country air."
The neighbor feels free
to help himself to apples now and again.
The man swears they are
the best apples he ever ate.

At tour's end, Dad shows how he
moved the stone path over a little
for Mom to make room for marigolds
at the edge, mocking
our concept of octogenarians.

"There are so many flowers,"
he says to me. "You must look
at them all—carefully!" His hearty laugh
trails down the path with him,
while I remain to ponder flowers.

The Spring

Effervescence flowing, Dad
observes, shapes, sprinkles roses
and carnations and his
prizewinning orchids brought out
on the patio from inside.

On intermittent trips into the house,
later on, he enters the world
of the new woodcut, window
on a boat yard in California,
whose boats gently sway on waves.

Passing the hall mirror, my father's
probing eyes startle me, he
having taught me to see.

I glance again, to make sure,
and they soften into my mother's
blue, she having taught me to read.

The River

Barefoot, I move from living room
carpet to warm patio concrete
and into moist grass,
feeling connected to my source.
The cardinal pair, sitting
on the ailing birch tree, give
confidence in life's constant renewal.
Sitting on the patio, I ponder
the two-fold nature of my existence.

Here I am in the world
where thoughts gather unimpeded,
where each sound is not distraction
but a part of the whole,
where the spring of life feeds the river
flowing into the sea of being.

Peace of Mind

Little by little
she retrieved fragments
of an anonymous self
invisible gifts
she had placed day by day
in different rooms of a house
He had built
the large rough cedar house
with too many doors
and dark hallways
He had consumed
generous meals
wanting more
She had
no answers
He asked
no questions
In the end
he kept
the dried roses
his name
the dark
empty house
a wall of green
and the blossomless rosebush
growing like a vine
She gathered
potted flowers
a desk
the pictures
and a wanting
to know more

brought them all out
into the sunshine
like mysteries
waiting for light